ON LOVE AND LIGHT IN A WORLD OF LOSS

KEVIN JAMES HESS

E&M

Eckhart & May
PO Box 255
Hannacroix, NY 12087
www.eckhartandmay.com

Copyright © 2024 by Kevin James Hess
Printed in the United States of America
Cover painting, "Steady Heart" by Theresa Utschig
ISBN 978-1-958061-96-1 | paper
ISBN 978-1-958061-97-8 | ePub

CONTENTS

Acknowledgments   ix
Introduction   xi

I Have a Fire   1
Sneaking In/Breaking   2
Half Life of a Mantle   3
Dreaming Of You   4
Butterfly   5
20 Years Ago   7
Tourniquet Today   9
Last Night at the Show   10
Hello Friend   11
Vocation, For Now   12
The Failure Of Man   13
Small Wonders   14
Slow and Relentless   15
Airplane Eucharist   16
Haverfeld Happiness   17
Acolytes   18
Forgiveness   19
For Now   20
Bird at Flight   21
Starhome   22
You Are My Prayer   23
Waiting   24
Ancient Beings   25
Making Our Way   26
Freija   27
Easter Sunday   28
100% (Not Yet Done)   29
Thoughts about Steps   30
Sharing/Take My Hand   31

Whenever	32
What I Found One Day	33
We Are Lost Until We Learn How to Ask	34
Snow Blown	35
One Month	36
An End of the Beginning	37
Ash	38
Do Well	39
Medium	40
On Courage and Trust	42
Peace	43
Kids Talking	44
Learning to Swing	45
Misunderstood	46
Moon House	47
One Possible Bite	48
So That's Done	49
Opening the Door	50
Princess (Territory Edit)	51
Summon the Soul	52
Sometime Later	53
Such Magic as You Have	54
Expansion	56
Exposed	57
Drawing a Blank	58
Draught	59
Defeating Dark	60
Darling, You Spend My Heart So Lavishly	61
Conflagration	62
Bury Me Black	63
Breathing	64
Bounded	65
Beauty	66
At Least At Last	67
The Beautiful Things	68
Another's Goodbye	69
Anger	71
And They Looked	72

Amorphous Blob   73
Alchemy   74
#819   75
Fill My Heart   76
Grouse Creek   77
Opening   78
New Day   79
Pumpkin Day   80
I Love You   81
Life Giving   82
Madame de Pompadour   83
O'erflown/Sampling Fog   84
Oblation   85
You Who Are   86

About the Author   87

To all who have loved and love
and feel the deep blessing, burden,
and call of Love in all its myriad forms.

To Elizabeth Suzanne Delaney Hess,
whose Love and Light I will always cherish.

To Liam Samuel Hess who is my raison d'être.
You are the greatest gift.

ACKNOWLEDGMENTS

My deep love and gratitude belong first and foremost to Wendy Michelle Cooper, MFA, who read, commented, and edited this volume, whose intuitive skills have activated so much healing in my life, and whose patience, inspiration, and generosity have shown forth a brilliant golden light to help illuminate my way on this journey. I love you, darling flower of life.

My heartfelt thanks to Carlyn Bland, MA, and Heidi Lynn Nilsson, MFA, who read and provided invaluable feedback on this volume, enabled me to turn some essential personal corners, and inspired me to run through the finish line.

My great respect is also due to The Solvang Writer's Group: Christie Yant, John Joseph Adams, Reece Michaelson, and Gary Robinson. You welcomed me, stood by me, challenged me, and encouraged me to strive for and manifest this dream. I cherish you all.

INTRODUCTION

This volume was born of love, pain, and grief. It represents a cumulation of reflections going back 20 or 25 years. Love in loss leads to either deep resentment or deep forgiveness. In these pages you will find both, sometimes stated clearly, sometimes messily so. But the words are only part of the story. Let their spirit move and resonate within you. It isn't really all that important whether you believe in a higher power or an existence beyond what we all experience in this realm of consciousness. Our hearts seem to know which way is North even when our minds reject it.

Most of these poems are a love letter to my own heart, a beseeching to greater understanding and compassion: a "befriending of my Self" as renowned Buddhist nun Pema Chödrön might put it. Polonius advises Laertes in Act 1 Sc III of Hamlet "This above all: to thine own self be true, And it must follow, as the night the day, Thou canst not then be false to any man." The words, images, and deep longings offered here reflect a world of deep disconnect but also one of simple knowing and of plainly held truths. I don't have all the answers, nor do I need them. In the end it turns out the only critical piece to this question of Love is whether I have the courage to love myself as I am, here and now. For so long, at least in the Christian tradition in which I was raised and spent several decades, YHWH was understood to mean 'I am that I am' when the original Hebrew is so much more dynamic: 'I am here, now!' Again, regardless of what we may believe about what may or may not exist beyond this frail and beautiful life of ours, we inevitably find common ground in the simple fact of the present moment—we are promised only right now, and that is ephemeral at best.

And that truth is in the end a deep and abiding gift: that we get to choose, moment by moment, how we will respond to the circumstances of our lives. We are not bound to ineffability. Instead we are free agents who can effect instantaneous change in our lives simply by being present to ourselves and to our lives.

I offer this volume humbly and without expectation. May you find hope and love and enlightenment in these passages, not through any craft or wisdom I here present, but through the resonance your own lived and loved truth reveals within you. Our interactions with one another are waypoints—sparks of love and light in a world of seemingly constant loss. What we find is that that loss is only the releasing of who we are not as we are revealed, moment by moment, in our choices to be here, and now, in Love.

I HAVE A FIRE

I have love in an overcrowded space
I have angels who guide me on this terrestrial plane
I have a body that allows me to feel grace
I can move mountains with just this heart of mine

The cold grey of outside is a pause in my day
Wait we have a new backdrop coming in
Life will not always be this way
You didn't come here just to stir a pot

Shake shit up. Excite hope. Stimulate anger to change
Repel dreamless dozing that golem creator
Stained glass marks our passing from truth to truth
Like an elephant's trunk swaying side to side

I am barely here sometimes just some ephemeral
Knowing in a body barely sensing of a love
That surrounds me fully transforms me mercifully
I have a fire burning in my hearth, unfurling my soul

SNEAKING IN/BREAKING

I am going to break you
Through nefarious means.

Pressing in as a paw to
Carpet I come.

Welcomed, you shepherd me
Here, direct me there.

I obey, and I watch,
and I learn your ways.

I hear your heart
I feel your force.

Circling 'round your soul,
A whispered breath am I.

Smooth wall, featureless form:
I am learning you.

You are learning to trust me
But I already love you.

HALF LIFE OF A MANTLE

I wrapped you about me some twenty plus years ago
As water wraps a rock airtight, not a bubble in sight

Caressing, smoothing, wearing, grooving
You taught me scansion
You gave me new vision
So many times I fell broken before you
And you stood there and said
Get the fuck up

A dusty barren bed lays around me now.
Only the histories this bare rock can tell remain
Learning to stand is a humbling proposition.
Building takes time.
We had a lifetime together. Roughly half of yours.
When I am done
Building the rest of mine I will set you on the mantle.

DREAMING OF YOU

Tonight was full of simple pleasures:
A little pot on the beach
A failed takeout followed by a bit of roaming
That finally manifested in sweet and sour.
I earlier today feared a sour end—I dare say
I deserved it after the last two days.
But your clarity of light opened my eyes,
Enabled me to renew my vision of myself.
The work I have had to do
to acknowledge my own worthiness
Shocks me when I would have claimed
I knew me from seed to tree.
Love perseveres in crafting me.
I'll say it again, I thought I knew love, then I met you.
Special does not satisfy, unique is too mundane.
You called me your soulmate.
Said you manifested me.
Five weeks in, the scales dropped,
my sight revisits each light.

BUTTERFLY

Love, you are my dream
You come to me open

Softly take me, hand cupped
In your hand, caress my soul

My me, so that I soften and
Flutter delicate as wings
Breezily flitted

I happen upon your gentle
Petite Polynesian nose-arch

Tickled you twitch,
Thrilling through

My me, so that I soften,
Flutter delicate as wings
Breezily flitted

I catch your effervescent eyes
With their lit smile

Tracking my movements
Quietly knowing

My me, so that I soften,
Flutter delicate as wings
Breezily flitted

Love, that you may dream
I come to you open

Softly take you, hand cupped
In my hand, caress your soul

20 YEARS AGO

On this day 20 years ago
we were quite possibly at Hengrave
causing nunstress or some other fucking thing.

On this day 20 years ago
we were almost certainly cold, with
73.4% chance of damp from an annoying drizzle.

On this day 20 years ago
we were writing papers too late at night,
rolling clementines down the hall.

On this day 20 years ago
we were snacking on cheese and salami
after some questionable dinner
...some things never change.

On this day 20 years ago
we avoided the Red Chamber because
the guys in there had turned it into a locker room.

On this day 20 years ago
Heather was still quite angry with you
for settling.

On this day 20 years ago
I really didn't know how lucky I was.

On this day 20 years ago

we were just back together after three
months, in which I ran up a hefty phone bill.

On this day 20 years ago
we could not imagine the blessing who is
Liam Samuel.

On this day 20 years ago
I wondered what I might be doing 20
years hence, and whether we would ever be back.

On this day 20 years ago
I was completely mesmerized by your
ability to articulate.

On this day 20 years ago

TOURNIQUET TODAY

I wore a tourniquet today
On my heart, nay my very soul.
Lost part of my mind—
It just escaped my hold.

Bonds of desperation wrapped
Tight but soaked through.
I watched myself losing
Me through my mind's eye.

Lips too taut to taste
Heart drifting off pulse,
Leg twitching agonized revolts,
And then I took a slow breath.

LAST NIGHT AT THE SHOW

I snuck in the side door...
The door everyone enters.
The front is jammed up:
Drunk Druidic dwarves

One mistook the façade
Diamonds! Diamonds!
Never has such a passel of fools
Been so bamboozled

By a placebo of cubic zirconia...
But hopeless hearts lead
All astray; annoyed, a passing crone
Turned all their parts to molding stone.

HELLO FRIEND

I do not know how to reach you.
I know you need a friend now.
Probably you have some rule that says no.

I know that you are hurting, and that you
are not caring for yourself nearly enough.

That you are communicating in code,
murky and incoherent.
That you need to deal with this loss.

That you need to be unstoppable.
That you must do.

When are you just you? The sermon must be done.
So much important ministry to accomplish.

When do you love you. When do you not do.
You have protected yourself, as we do.

I am calling to you. Here. Now.
Be.

Don't think.
Don't examine, analyze, or respond.

Breathe, and let love in...

VOCATION, FOR NOW

I may be stuck in a dualism.

I love. I hate.
I dream. I despair.
I move forward and back in the same step
Without a hope for change, for change is ever present.

I love you. You don't want me to say those words.
For you it isn't true. To speak them would be cruel.
But you care for me.
So carefully planned are your steps.
Aware of everything I say or do near you.
Like a ninja you know

                    my every move.

Maybe love = obsession in this stupid game.
Is my vocation obsession and you are my latest pawn?
How do I quit you?
How can any hope still ring true.

THE FAILURE OF MAN

Looking on your face I dream
Of times I wish to be.
For you I wish to do everything.

Because you. Because you.
Because I said this once before, before you, before
I have sworn there could be no more.

Betrayed by my choices,
by my heart, by my weakness for
acceptance.
I have broken that which is most precious to me.
To satisfy that which is most precious to me.

SMALL WONDERS

You were the only one there. My hope and fear.
I had already been and gone and come again.

A vision of joy you were, bright as morning dew.
And I, I had a key, though what all it unlocks

Has not yet been told true. Syncopation obfuscates;
The gaps we feel, beats left unfelt.

And yet we hear them anyway,
In our hearts

SLOW AND RELENTLESS

If hope is to be found,
If illegitimate dreams,
If you, what horrible

Tragedies must transpire?
Am I a monster
Because such thoughts
Bubble up?

Maybe. Maybe if I ignore them
They will lose interest.
The Buddha says
"Don't believe everything you think."

And I feel lost
But my belief tells me
All will be well
And all manner of things will be well.

And so I pray

AIRPLANE EUCHARIST

Sparkling resonances flow back
Here's one here's another tonic
Mottled hexagonal vainglory grins full frontal lack;
Pale truth bares redemption a cracker,
Confident smile.
Cocoa charm slumbers, ten teal ends
Dispense apportioned recompense and
Visage now sated.
For the rest heavenly oblation, chittered incantations,
rejuvenation;
Mutually accepted disconnection.
Land

HAVERFELD HAPPINESS

The loss is real.
The pain is too.
The desperation floods.
The rage pounds.

The only thing I can't believe is how I feel.

ACOLYTES

20 years on
She is gone

But her children love on:
One she birthed,

The rest were formed -
As of memory clay.

Each found her own path,
Opened her own heart;

Filled her own head,
Shared her own wisdom;

Bestowed her own love,
Freely or judiciously;

And each is remarkable in her own right,
But none can know as she knew,

None can understand what she understood,
None can see the depths she saw.

Can I forgive a world that no longer recognizes me?
Can I be forgiven by a world I do not now understand?

FORGIVENESS

I have broken my heart not to break yours.
I have broken my heart, when will it mend?

Who can know this, whose strength sustains?
Don't tell me god, I have not his ears here.

And if I turn away, this all goes away.
You are no fool. But if known then you are also cruel.

What recompense would you ask, if you knew?
Or would you simply turn, heart and soul?

I have a hopeless heart. I got scared.
I am a cowardly fool.

Hell is Here and Now.
Sirens, and I wholly entranced.

FOR NOW

If there were no cares to care, no boxes to check...

They stood upon the craft,
A worthy vessel of the sea.

Bobbing through glimpses of starlit waves—
"We could stay here forever," they mused

"We're in between this and that,
And here and there.

Nothing drives us forth
Nothing beckons us back."

They had been blessed by a shaman on their departure;
A priest said she'd pray each day.

The GPS tracks them
And the weather satellite warns them

But they still felt free to roam
Because they had nowhere to be.

"Dream a little dream, Darling,
And here we are, stepping into an ever-new dawn."

BIRD AT FLIGHT

Blustering winds meet joy of life.
Strength of wing and purpose of mind.

A cat played with Ravel and Ravel flew.
Flit. Flitter. Flittering.

Air of love. Love of air.
Note. Notes. Noting.

Eddy. Breeze. Gust. Eddy.
Tempo. Reflex. Feel.

Finger or key.
Feather or flow.

Nothing above.
Nothing below.

A tear drops.
Thus begins a lake below.

STARHOME

The home of my stars
Is Starhome, in my heart.
They are enfleshed;
I release them at will

And project my light,
The orbits of my life
For all who would see,
To show all who know me.

I live a small life
But my stars burn through
Night and strife and shite—
Find yourself by them.

One day these sparkling gems
Will align, unlock the door,
And reveal to me
What I was born for.

YOU ARE MY PRAYER

Little bit by little bit;
Touch by smile by passing wave
I know you though I don't know
Quite how I do.

I suppose I've taken in a few things
Along the way. I feel your gentle care
Though I may not see you for days;
Then, I revisit your words like a prayer.

Yes, they are my prayer. I lift them up,
release them to the heavens, and try
Not to hope. I trust instead.
Trust is a new friend in my life,

One I don't know very well
But who looks a lot like you.
Touch by smile by passing wave
You know me, you trust me, you love me.

WAITING

I breathe, slowly: in, out, in, out
I breathe, aware of so many doubts
I breathe, filling the sail of my little boat
I breathe, where you were echoes' loss
I breathe, releasing my tears
I breathe a kiss, your eyelids would crinkle
I breathe but do not wait for there is no return
I breathe because you cannot
I breathe your breath, your life is within me

ANCIENT BEINGS

They may not exist
According to our scientific records
Rules of our road
Civilization having decided how
Even when they enter my dreams
I fight against the poverty in my soul
It's not enough to simply light a fire
The wind and the waves and ocean spray
My pocket Merkabah links me to truth
And I spend money on you

MAKING OUR WAY

Come shadow lark come
Teach us the song of home.
Tease out our notes with a patient draw:
Trill and warble, woo loop and caw.

Fear would stay our searching, distract our choices:
Flit? Swoop? Titter?...Hop? Scurry? Poise?
We know not whence we came
Nor whither we go;
each wonders and wanders the same.

Search this soul as the cacophonous depths of night
My compass was set against some imperfect starlight.
Choose any hope, you have why
To hand—heart dares not now lie.

It was how I got lost at the start
Some wayward note did seem to fit this heart.
Come, shadow lark, come
Lead us now to our songs' true home...

FREIJA

Felt need;
A depth of lossless
Hope.

Hidden countenance:
Saplings sun,
Rooting to life.

Of somnolent
Haberdashery
Conventions

Deconstructed,
Dematerialized,
Demystified,

Feathers waft
From Spring's flourishing
Maypole.

Some days will end this way
While others
A sacred omen will keep

EASTER SUNDAY

I'm sitting in her service
Listening to her hymns
Visualizing her face

That of Botticelli
...we will rejoice ♪♪
Her breast lifts buoyant

Cerulean orbs
Shot with lightning
Crosses turn ashen

How do we mark death
In the thresholds of our lives
Do we let death mark us instead?

Stand fast to solid, dead hopes
Or step into the loss
Shaking and wobbly

Release our grasp
Deprecate hope to midden
Liberation remains

Still in her service sublime
Her hymns ebb and flow
Her coursing life a piquant love

100% (NOT YET DONE)

The very land towers above me.
A great pouring forth of self:
Some great showering faith
Which was not separated from time.

The slivering inverted land yields to our inquiries;
Not yielding itself to knowing
Stairs to nowhere
Stairs to You-know-where

Brightness foreshadowing dawn
Forestalling sight lines up
Rushing crushing cold
Clear cacophony

Verdant hope of
Green waste
Shear faith of possibility
Stamina of the soul

THOUGHTS ABOUT STEPS

When I think of you
I dream of what could be
I think I always have
Eyes to horizon

Do I hear you?
Do I love you?
What do I want?
Who am I?

You are practical
You are what you do
You say
You

I smile at the thought
What is next?
Where will I go?
Who will I be?

And I hear you say
The horizon is
Here
Now

SHARING/TAKE MY HAND

Come, let us journey together
In parallel to one another's grief and joy
and heartfelt hopes.

We don't have to speak of them,
only acknowledge they are there.
All I ask is to toil alongside you for a little while.

WHENEVER

Whenever I smile
I have a reason:
Someone
Something
Somewhat
Befriended
By a small joy, a temporary boon.

A broken bay leaf floats by.

WHAT I FOUND ONE DAY

Somehow there you were
Just standing there, treasure
Unsought-after
But needed desperately

I cry at my luck that night
But it wasn't luck it was love
Open, gentle, assured
Strong as any hope

A friend of a friend
Taking chances, playing the odds
I was never any good at poker
Playing mercy for a fool

Errand that had no outcome
Momma used to ask me where my head was
In the clouds, in the clouds
Mercy, my love, Gaia feels my feet once again

WE ARE LOST UNTIL WE LEARN HOW TO ASK

A lifted line
An appropriated thought
A need that needs us
To even exist

We need to be needed
The lagoon needs the swimmer to know
how beautiful it is
The berry bush needs the bear
to be truly worthy of its great
offerings
Our love must be received, not just desired

SNOW BLOWN

Flakes of perfection
Fall to abandon it all
Mere moments later

ONE MONTH

At the beginning of this year
I ended your life.
The law, the doctors, the slight trembling in my heart
Said it was alright.

Your body had been broken for weeks already,
Your mind flooded with lifeblood.
The only return was slavery.
The only way forward was loss.

I relieved you of the only life you have ever known
Watched as your body
took its last deep, beautiful breaths
Birthing your soul into a great and glorious unknown
Blessing you with freedom

AN END OF THE BEGINNING

Open to receive
When what has been given is a virus
A thing so small as to be indistinguishable to sight
A thing so counter to our own selves as to damage us
We don't have hope we have fixes, and plans, and tests
To separate, repel, and destroy the invader
A thing we have likely created
in the course of civilization

Open to receive
And our gift to ourselves is planetwide reset. Stop.
Listen to ourselves
Hear wholeness
Underneath the patterning
The raging inferno
Generations of loss
Remorse chucked on pile
Like so much garbage
We don't know how to factor

Open to receive
Love is loss is life
Is this what we are about
Or do we pine for something more
Can the unholiness of our desires be purified
Can our brokenness be taken apart
And shown to be whole
A beauty magnificent and extant

ASH

Reflection on Joel Gunderson's 'Song for Ashes'

Ash is pervasive, clinging to whatever it touches. And
loss, hurt, grief. And longing, hope, desire. Ash is life.
Life feeds ash.

Ash describes the past only, a reminder of what the
future can never hold. The lightest millstone, ash can
never be overcome.

But some brilliant soul invented a dustpan to collect
the past and make space for life, bright as a sun,
unfathomable as a phoenix.

Ash must be. Ash must be left behind. Ash is silence
after the song is done. Without ash there is no song;
without loss there is no life.

DO WELL

You show us what it means to be open-hearted
You show us what it means to be in our light
You show us safety, support, self-love
You teach your life
You practice your passion
You live your truth in the finest transparency
Your revenge is love
Your respite is hope
Your dream is healing
Your love is your life
You are that you are and
You are the gift God has given us

MEDIUM

Between you and me and some great heraldry
a layer lies
Soft and unseen, though felt keenly in the thin spaces.

You press in and I enfold, drawing us together as one.
I sense your coming and going, know your heart home,

The way your energy spikes for readings,
How you drift slowly off in the crook of my arm.

Our lips melt at touch, contours commingling.
I want to tell you how I loved you right from the start—

Where I met your soft Southern accent
and my heart fluttered.
Of the constant netting required since,

Since back then I was not but a name on your roster.
When Spirit spoke I listened, and heard your heartbeat
syllable by syllable,

Crafting layers of rhythm,
Bonding our hearts in a sudden sublime rhyme.

You've read my soul unfiltered,
You've lit my life with golden light.

My drifting days are done,

soil tending now my bonded trade.
Let me dock in your hallowed harbor,
and feed your soul my love.

ON COURAGE AND TRUST

I used to believe my faith defined me, and
Having no real faith I was therefore nothing. I
Lived this way for years. That's a misnomer. I
Died this way for years. Depression was my
Constant companion, I my own jailer. I cried
I raged I despaired I concluded that I wasn't a thing.
I had to lose what I loved most to let go of myself
That I loved least. Relinquishing the black dream
Renewed my heart. Letting go of "god" I suddenly
Had room in my heart for Love.

PEACE

Like a river flows, downstream to that great ocean
For that is where our ease is in our hearts,

Where Jesus calls us home, not to Heaven—
Some fancy mansion of white marble
and gleaming gold

But to our hearts, here and now and human.
Peace, like a river, flows—unless we dam it

Or rend it midair like a dove
struggling the hawk's talons.
Peace, like a river flows, unless we piss in it

With our bile and revenge and rightness.
Peace, like a river of blood we can't tide
'cause we've let it,

But peace, a child dreaming of
lambs, fields, and butterfly wings,
Where my Love awaits me,
in our secret meadow by the shore.

Peace

KIDS TALKING

A horn is indiscriminately blaring offense,
Water babbles in the fountain's electric loop,
And Saturday afternoon slumbers by.
Our fence is knocked from time to time
from the other side.
It's more of a whomp really;
a six-year-old body thump.
High-pitched voices carry in the wind,
Bringing news of the moment,
Only to be forgotten in my next breath.
A pair of baby blues peep over the fence;
I meet them from across the yard, holding the moment
Before they slide surreptitiously back down,
Oblivious I had been conversing with my lawn
leprechaun Henry
about red clover.

LEARNING TO SWING

I haven't got it, not on my own
Life is overwhelming to say the least.
I rely on Joy and Love, my old friends.
Gratitude is my watchword to recall:
Apples, kisses, the rub of a cat's fur
As he nestles by me seeking attention.

I burned a dozen dried roses this morning they
Were beautiful. They were beautiful living too
When I gave them to my wife. Laid
Them across her car actually, after having been an ass.
Long stems with vibrant fragrant blooms.
Made her cry.

I burned a dozen roses this morning they
Were sad drooping blooms. Dried that way. I
Bought them for my wife when she was
In hospital not recovering from a failed
Successful surgery. Her courage was inescapable.
My grief incalculable.
They lit up in a bonfire of grief and release.

I burned a couple roses today. Don't even remember
When or what they were from.
Smelled the best of the lot.
Must have been a happier time. A time past.
A time yet to come.
A time here.
And now.

MISUNDERSTOOD

It feels endless
I consider myself
I offer my clarity
I am read wrong

How does the translation
Undergo such a transformation
Transference fear
Failure of freedom

But what if my love language
Is a language of fear for you
If my heart is your hurt
Where can truth come in

MOON HOUSE

Moon over my house
Who do you speak to
At night, in the starlight?

Do the streetlights call
To you in hopes of reply?
We too shine like stars.

A new constellation: boxes,
Lines, and situated urbanity—
The conversation goes on

But soon circles back. You are no Pleiades,
Nor Capricorn; Zeus knows not your
Provenance, nor God your map.

Ah, but we are placed by the new gods
Whose ancestors named you, framed you,
Imbued you with meaning.

Perhaps they have tired of touching only thought,
And now seek light for their grasping fingers,
Tremulous in their control.

ONE POSSIBLE BITE

When I think about decadent desserts
cheesecake comes to mind
Before chocolate fudge tort
Ahead of mixed berry sorbet
Easily outstripping the cheese plate

I think of a thick, warm blueberry compote
And a decorative chocolate plate adornment
All of which quickens my pulse and slows my eyes
Chocolate, blueberries, cream cheese, cake, flooding
my mouth

Like love
Like a slow-motion supernova
Everything extraneous rejected

Only core truths are tasted and tested
Exultant existence emerges
Quiddity pulsing like a quasar for a time
Before all life extirpates or separates

SO THAT'S DONE

Quantum Healing.
Quantum quackery?
I'll leave it to you, dear reader, to decide for yourself.
But as for me I believe.
I have felt the end.
I longed for it.
Prayed for it.
Even contemplated enacting it.
But the truth is I found it a cowardly approach.
But the greater truth is I was living in death.
I was dying not living.
Aching not breathing.
Grieving not loving.
Weeping not rejoicing.
I know not how.
I have no need to know.
How I know is how I feel.
I am that I am.
I need acknowledge to no one but me.
I require no explanation be given to you.
I opened my heart and trusted it true.

OPENING THE DOOR

Sometimes we get stuck. Or lost in a
Space we don't know what to do with.
Just suddenly there is no ground in front of
You, and turning around is simply admitting
Defeat. And forward you don't know how to
Cross. Reach down and open the door in the
Void before you. Don't look just grab hold and pull.

PRINCESS (TERRITORY EDIT)

Her ferocious love rives my heart
Into her arms my ribbons fall
Layer upon layer every color of life
The hues of love splash forth
Commingling, twisting a braid
Transforming my life into
The bond that will never break

SUMMON THE SOUL

Celebrate life within you
Give oblation to your heart
Lead with what fires your belly
Love the thing sweating your palms

Speak with your voice lifted up to your heights
Homage your heart of hearts
without obligation or reservation
For none can be you and you alone are truly you
Give love give love give love

SOMETIME LATER

I opened a door
You walked through
Hope, intuition, tarot
Acrobatics of the heart
Shape-shifting as a start
When I open my eyes
I see only the golden dawn of you

SUCH MAGIC AS YOU HAVE

A guitar plays in the background,
Beyond the wood, across the butterfly divide.
Cords riff, tripping through branch and moss.

You are posting about wildflowers
And spirit and the frequency of bees.
I stare at the blue paint graffiti decorating

A long since fallen log upon which I sit.
Which message of frustration led this child to grief?
It means nothing to the ant
wandering its wayward path.

It seems boring to me,
now seeing a monochromatic diatribe.
I can't talk to the grief and I hear only muted relief.
A rustle in the nearby bush reveals a skunk
foraging for dinner.

A small, clear voice.
In the clearing it notices us, sniffs.
We meet eye to eye.

You ask what to do.
I suggest we do nothing.
The skunk, disinterested after the briefest of hellos,
rustles on.

You continue channeling.

My butt is starting to get sore on this log.
Light wanes ever so slightly,
just enough to catch my eye.

I know you'd want the purple water bottle.
I'm glad.
My lavender shirt is no match for your blazing violet
heart.

EXPANSION

Broaching my heart
Is a trip.

One moment as fearsome
As another is droll.

Fainting in a field of poppies;
Feinting from myself.

Wine unwound me once,
Now love keeps inflating my universe.

EXPOSED

I have opened my heart.
I am trying not to expect
That which I have no right
To expect, but my heart

It beats erratically when you are
near to me. My breath catches.
I have to consciously withhold autonomic
reach.

You spoke once of seeing but a fleeting glimpse,
light that shows us a vision of the future, and
Fades from our view.
If we are to know the truth we must follow the

Light that was, trusting it still is.
My heart is open, having felt the glow
Of you, not knowing where it will go,
What path it leads to.

DRAWING A BLANK

My canvas is covered with paint.
Oil pinnacles give topology to an unmapped landscape.
I have lost track of the color wheel,
Numbers were never my strong suit.

The delicate nuance of white, green, and blue
That give life to a wave as it crests
Just before the plunge.
There you will find my heart beating,

Surging just below the surface.
Never seen, pulsing in unison
To the masterstrokes of a
Quantum conductor.

You navigate these waters,
know them better than I do.
Though perhaps I am climbing the
Mast blindfolded yet again.

DRAUGHT

Slow and relentless.
Drifting silvan presence
But spritely you appear
To all around.

Plenipotentiary of one
Precious world. Only a small space
But inhabit it you do; full of life
Lived, uncompromising and true.

A bird cracked its neck today, fighting itself;
Window wins. I do not fear death you said.
Nor should you; nor should anyone.
But can you bear to live with love once more?

DEFEATING DARK

My mind's eye is lit, but darkly—
Anxiety from last night I let stay over
Like a one-night stand
That I only remember too late,
That won't go quietly or particularly willingly.

But I find they aren't fond of jazz—
Narrowest of cracks and like water
The melancholy has no choice but to run.
I breathe the freed air deep,
Delicious rhythms of joyeria and santo.

DARLING, YOU SPEND MY HEART SO LAVISHLY

I align with the star of you. My compass holds true—
North, East, South, West makes no difference.

I burn and I burn and you thaw by my fire,
Fear, conceit, self-repulsion from my increasingly
supple frame.

You call me to account with palpable love.
I took a leap in trusting you. I don't know

What faith I had but I went all in.
My only fear was not leaping.

And that one decision has burst my
Heart wide open. My failures are my own.

But my Love
My love is made manifest in you.

CONFLAGRATION

My mouth opens silence fills the hollow
where words would be.
My eyes drink in the disaster
of your machine-coddled body;
Everything there, just vacant.
My hands touch you but you are cold,
your fire has gone out.

Or rather, it was sucked out by the great wash of hot
blood the surgeons say coursed through your brain; a
raging conflagration of your life that left nothing but a
dead, gray lump in its wake.

Through this precious landscape I now roam.

BURY ME BLACK

Sweep across my shores tonight.
Slip and tack draw me in.
Catch my fancy then drip my dreams
drop at a time 'til I am dry,

Swept clean of my debris
and ready for the next round.
Willingly the cogs turn true
up, around, and it's all profound:

Haveland nederpose upskrilled!
So many heads are spinning,
longings churning as we drain
away, channeled through testy

Angles, all simpering sloshes
that might chance an escape should we
Catch a whiff of the sea: sweetness
only rushing brine can bring

To some dried out old visage.
Sweep across my shores this night,
draw me out drop by loving drop
and I will break your long clock.

BREATHING

In this Moment,
When I am in love,
When the pain smarts,
When my heart charts
Every jot and tittle,
I lay myself before
You and I rejoice.
This is living.

BOUNDED

We are floating lifelines.

To one another we stretch.

From the Other comes hope,
Newness, option, disparity.

Wilted zeal tempts our dreams.

Temptation steals our smiles
And binds our Sisyphean fears.

BEAUTY

What a beauty you are!
Glorious and gracious,
Brilliant and bold,
Caring and careful.
Adjectives for miles,
And truth powers each.
If I didn't know better
I'd say you were me
And I was you.
Mirrors don't lie, kid.

AT LEAST AT LAST

L'écureuil est mort

I've finally lost
That which I never held.
There is such clarity in silence;
You owe me nothing,

Never have, not a thing.
But how I've hoped like a fool:
I've lost my soul,
But maybe I'm rematerializing?

It's so hard
To hear myself
through the storm
Of my incessant attention-seeking—

Was there ever anything else?
But that is a selfish question
For another day, and
Another soul. Not mine

THE BEAUTIFUL THINGS

Night sky right now
How cold I am
Your huge heart
My broken parts

Breezy palms
Silhouetted stars
Tandem rockers
Liam, all fresh

Lilting tunes
Discovering England
Discovering you
Haunting truths

Am I bored
Or tired
Or scared
Or true

ANOTHER'S GOODBYE

What can I say at this passing?
So little do I know that
meets you keeps you protects you.

What hope is there in such pain—
Raw open final unspeakable unknowable desperate
untouchable.

Vanquished dreams, welled grief, blooded rage,
Unthinkable awareness.

Nay unconscionable nay unknowable
Nay undreamable nay unnightmareable.

Spirit swirl, gather you up, touchless—wafting—
drawing out your raw-hearted grief
when acceptance is the only possible balm.

To heal is not a distance you could ever cover
Heed this breached landscape you must;
no bridge may reach.

What can I say or do or dream or hope for you
I mean nothing in this deathly equation;
reduce to none.

Where is your heart in between
back then and the heedless now of

Standing by incapacitated by what is; can never be;
should have—

There can be no complete goodbyes.
There is nothing, nothing as final as nothingness.

We must only start out again, bearing also this truth.
Not new, nor renewed, but not alone.

ANGER

I woke angry. I woke lonely. I bawled.
I woke needing you and you aren't here.
It's not you. It's not me. It's us. We are pacing.
And I don't like to wait. I want it and I want it now.
Where the fuck did that come from?
Actually, who cares.
Let the therapists figure that one out. Let me be.
I released anger I have held against family.
I still held anger
I have unjustly manifested against you.
And I was warned. Twice. I didn't listen.
And I broke when you called.
I snapped and blamed you.
And I was wrong. Well, not wrong, wrong to accuse.
I blamed you for a joint conundrum. A shit we share.
I need you. I want you. I can get on without you.
Trust is something we are both still working on.
My anger, my impatience,
my loneliness are all faithless.
I set an intention to trust you, eyes wide,
gazing into yours.

AND THEY LOOKED

My heart, opened, was filled with nectar
from the soul of the
wind.

The bloom was fast upon me
Heart full, blessed with life and vitality.
Fruit ripens fast in the sun when water and soil
abound.

But who will pick such fruit? Who can?
Where does authority rest to harvest what
The soul of the wind has brought?

I am but a vessel, an open receptacle. Do I
Close myself to truth? To love? Shall I be
Damned for fertility?

I close myself to the wind, let it pass me by.
There can be no more entry. But then do I die?

AMORPHOUS BLOB

Three classes online
Plus online training in financials
Apartment shopping
Kid home constantly
Covid kills for thrills
Not enough work
Not enough dough
Not enough blow
A love seat is in order, maybe
I want a wood tree that just pops off wood to burn
I wanna know what my life is about
I gave up anger before lent
So I can't bitch and moan for 6 weeks straight
and feel great
I envision myself a billionaire
In a Tesla
With a driver
And a pilot
And a transporter
Because fuck Science Fiction
I am here and now and Kevin

ALCHEMY

I sang a song once to a snake who was slithering by.
The snake turned to me and spoke:
Look to the sky, starseed; lend me your eye.
Your home is just there between the moon and the
things that make you cry.

I opened my heart and a new life popped out,
Just in time—right as my old life died.
A mix of truth and fiction had long
Kept me alive. But my love runs only on

Golden Light; I can no longer see
By any other frequency. I look to your hope,
I step forward in faith, I dream my truth,
And sink deep into the ground of being.

#819

I was warned, but still I listened as
Curiosity and Arrogance whispered "Savior."
I peered too long into light beyond my sight,
And managed to tear the veil of my oeuvre.

Heart-questions are not meant
for unsanctioned access;
I pried open another's sheltered shattered truths,
And laid bare my own in the process.

FILL MY HEART

Fill my heart with love
Like they do in the movies
Like the storybooks dream about
Like it once was—

Before the weight
Before the commitment
Before the yeses fired slugs,
Pierced my heart, spilled my soul.

Leaden I feel, drug down,
Trading places with fleeing air.
As midnight approaches
And possible truths

Fade away focus has no turn
To make. If wishes live, they
Live here, as my life seeps
Sticky drips I'd rather keep.

GROUSE CREEK

We didn't know what we were looking for,
But we knew what we wanted.

Liam compared maps and terrain as I drove,
Winding our way down into Yosemite Valley.

That one's too far down. That one's dead.
Mosquito Creek? Um, no. Gross!

And then we saw it. The perfect spot.
I pulled off the road and we watched

A ranger drive by, slow and intentional. We waited.
Scrabbling down the frozen embankment

I felt like a kid again, exploring the edge of reason.
Snow-crisp water splashed and gurgled, wending

Its way around Nature's deposit of rocks and
Twigs and fallen leaves. I suddenly couldn't

Speak. What could I possibly add to perfection?
In our hearts you will never float away.

OPENING

Split apart a heart encrusted,
Barnacled in hurt. Slip in,
Blade betwixt unwilling scabs.

And twist.

Fresh Love seeps out

NEW DAY

Good morning bunny, how warm you must be
In that fancy fur coat of yours.

I'm sorry, I know I am crossing your home;
Somebody poured this path years ago—
though I walk it now.

Matins. The space between the nether of the mind
And the heart of the day. Where we are soft and the air

Sharp, scraping cheeks and nipping nose.
But your nose just
Twitches, unperturbed save by me,
who travels this way

Every other day, on my way back to where I started.
See you later, bunny. Be warm and I will try to stay soft.

PUMPKIN DAY

Happy screeches, you know the kind.
Timid stares, grabby fingers, fangy faces,
All imbued with a common desire.

I LOVE YOU

Damn I'm in so much trouble
I know I haven't been playing pretend
But waking at 3:40 in the am pinned
To your reality shot my eyes wide

I don't know you, really
But I feel you, soully
Everything I know just defenestrated
Are you impatient? No, just sure

LIFE GIVING

When roley-poley
Crosses my path I step out
So it doesn't close

MADAME DE POMPADOUR

It's as if I was born to love you.
Some personality lineup;
Some characteristic chemistry.
But for cards you refuse to show

I would claim fait accompli,
But that's just me: believing w/o
Seeing, filling in gaps with hope
Born of some desperate dream.

Running from or running to
It would always be you
But here we go; you hither,
Me yon. You cannot help me, nor I you.

I have walked outside the boundaries
Again it would seem. Not in terms
Of you and me but in terms of me and me:
You are not the first nor the last.

You are the thread that is in me,
The hook that holds me fast.
Writers talk of what-if and
I am a lousy liar.

O'ERFLOWN/SAMPLING FOG

Low-lying bright white clouds spread thick
Folding sharply across the coast's corners
Sea just below, me high above
Reminds me of roughly spread frosting
The kind you can secretly swipe a finger through

OBLATION

Offer again
Returned undeliverable

Thinking ahead
I think

Communicate
They say

Listen better
They don't

Not really
Not meaningfully

A pelican flies over my heart
Daily delivery

Return to sender
Unremarkable
Unrequited

Unheard
Unbelievably
Unbalanced
Unbearable
Undelivered:
no accountability exists to receive your message

YOU WHO ARE

You yourself and nobody else
But you are called to be the nothing
Release all that you claim to be
Empty your heart of expectation
Clear your mind of demand
Fire the imagination

About the Author

Kevin James Hess was born in the South, raised in the West, and has now settled in Northern Wisconsin with his love, a psychic kitty, and a star kitten. A lifelong writer, English major, and graduate of the Indigo Lotus School of Intuitive Arts, after a too-long career in IT Kevin is now aligned to where he belongs—among nature, auroras, water, and words.